Gathering the Wind:

What the Bible Says About God, the Weather, and Climate Change

By Michael Galloway

ISBN-13: 978-0-9847402-3-9

www.michaelgalloway.net

Contents

"Who has ascended into heaven, or descended? Who has gathered the wind in His fists? Who has bound the waters in a garment? Who has established all the ends of the earth? What is His name, and what is His Son's name, if you know?"- Proverbs 30:4

- 1 -

Who Controls the Weather?

"The earth is the Lord's, and all its fullness, the world and those who dwell therein. For He has founded it upon the seas, and established it upon the waters." - Psalm 24:1-2

In the spring of 1873, farmers in southwestern Minnesota watched in concern as dark, whirling clouds appeared on the horizon. As the clouds approached, their appearance changed and soon they were accompanied by a rustling, screeching sound. This storm did not involve rain or wind, but instead was made of swarms of grasshoppers.

Within weeks, acre upon acre of crops lay devastated, and by 1877, over two-thirds of the state was battling the infestation. The grasshoppers even began devouring clothes left on clotheslines. Farmers tried everything from burning their crops to dragging pieces of sheet metal coated in tar or molasses through the fields to catch the pests. The sheet metal was then cleaned by putting the grasshoppers into a fire. Eventually, some of the farmers left altogether while others fought on despite discouraging odds.

After the manmade efforts to stop the devastation failed, Governor John S. Pillsbury declared a statewide day of prayer on April 26th, 1877. A massive sleet storm soon arrived and killed off many of the adult grasshoppers. Although the remaining eggs hatched, by September of that year, they had flown away and left the state for good.

Was this truly a miraculous act of God? If you subscribed to the clockwork universe theory, which was held by many scientists of that time, the answer would have been no. According to that theory, the universe is compared to a mechanical clock would up initially by God but now governed by the laws of physics. Local weather events then were merely a part of a larger, predictable system set in motion by God eons ago. In other words, the sleet storm was just a natural, perhaps cyclical, event.

Is God unconcerned and distant from His creation as this theory suggests? When it comes to weather, the Bible paints a different and more complicated picture. For example, in Matthew 8:23-27, we see Jesus and His disciples run into a bit of trouble while out in a boat:

"Now when He got into a boat, His disciples followed Him. And suddenly a great tempest arose on the sea, so that the boat was covered with the waves. But He was asleep. Then His disciples came to Him and awoke Him, saying, 'Lord, save us! We are perishing!' But He said to them, 'Why are you fearful, O you of little faith?' Then He arose and rebuked the winds and the sea, and there was a great calm. So the men marveled, saying, 'Who can this be, that even the winds and the sea obey Him?'"

Likewise, in the Book of Jonah we learn of a prophet who tried to flee from Lord's call. Jonah was told by God to deliver a message to the city of Nineveh, but instead he boarded a ship bound for Tarshish and fled. As a result, God then stirred up a storm on the sea. The sailors on board panicked and eventually Jonah informed them that the storm was his fault. In an act of self-sacrifice, he then let them throw him overboard and into the sea. The storm ceased, and Jonah was then swallowed by a "great fish" for three days. After a prayer, he was delivered back to land and given a second chance to deliver the message.

In a similar act of control over water, God also parted the Red Sea so that the Israelites could flee Egypt at the expense of the Egyptian army (see Exodus 14:13-28). Although these particular Biblical events are memorable and frequently cited as examples of how God has controlled the weather in the past, to many they appear as dramatic, once-in-history type miracles that will never be repeated again.

One Time or For All Time?

It's easy to look at these portions of Scripture and fall into the tendency to think God's only purpose here was to make a dramatic point. A closer look, however, reveals God is much more involved in the weather than the clockwork universe theory suggests, for instance. There are hundreds of verses in the Bible that refer to the weather or show God's direct intervention in the affairs of mankind through it. The purpose of the intervention is identical to the themes found elsewhere in the Bible: to show He is God, to warn people, to change the tide in battle, to show blessing, or in some cases, to execute judgment.

In Amos 4:13, it states "For behold, He who forms mountains, and creates the wind, who declares to man what His thought is, and makes the morning darkness, who treads the high places of the earth—the LORD God of hosts is His name." In Genesis 7:4 and Genesis 8:2, God turns the rain on and off to start and stop the most devastating flood that mankind has ever seen. Yet the concept of God controlling the rain as a means of blessing or judgment can also be found in Leviticus 26:4, Deuteronomy 11:14 and in other places. A lack or abundance of rain can have a significant impact on a nation, especially when in comes to agriculture as these verses point out.

In Job 37:11-12, God is described as having control over the clouds. It states, "Also with moisture He saturates the thick clouds; He scatters His bright clouds. And they swirl about, being turned by His guidance, that they may do whatever He commands them on the face of the whole earth." (Job 37:11-12) In Luke 23:45, during Jesus' crucifixion, the sun was described as being "darkened, and the veil of the temple was torn in two." Upon Christ's return, there will also be more signs in the sun, moon, and stars (see Luke 21:25 and Revelation 6:12). Although these signs can be visible to many at once, there still is this tendency to pass them off as routine events in the heavens, often in regard to eclipses of the sun and moon.

Bolts From the Blue

A while back, I watched a video taken from the International Space Station as it orbited around the Earth. Around the 22-second mark in the video, there are bursts of lightning from storms occurring on the surface of the planet that appear like fireflies caught in a spider web. From above, the view is amazing, but down below each bolt of lightning can reach temperatures of up to 50,000 degrees Fahrenheit and stretch up to five miles in length.

Although the space station video is fascinating, it also brings to mind Job 37:3 which reads, "He sends it forth under the whole heaven, His lightning to the ends of the earth." Along with this verse, in Job 38:35, God tells Job, "Can you send out lightnings, that they may go, and say to you, 'Here we are!'?" In Job 36:32, it reads, "He covers His hands with lightning, and commands it to strike." If God can command such elements as wind, rain, clouds, the sun and even individual lightning bolts, then what does this mean for us here on earth?

Although there have been many headlines of weather events as of late that are considered "epic" or even "of Biblical proportions", these verses do not imply that every single component of these events are a result of judgment for something or another. In later chapters I'll cover how God has used a weather event as a warning, a blessing, and even a means of judgment, but for now it's evident that God can and will use such means as necessary.

Praying For Rain

Earlier in this chapter I mentioned a call for a statewide day or prayer in response to a grasshopper plague. While the Bible makes it clear that God has ultimate control over the weather, is there any precedent for intervention in a situation like this one? As it turns out, there are plenty of examples. The first place we can look is I Samuel 12:18, where Samuel the prophet called upon the Lord, who in turn sent thunder and rain. At the time the Israelites complained about the lack of a king over them, even though God made it clear to them earlier that He was to be their king. Nevertheless, the Lord relented and Samuel anointed a king, but also made it clear to the people that God was still the one truly in charge.

Another example can be found in Exodus 9:22-23, when God directed Moses to stretch out his staff over the land of Egypt. Like the other plagues before and after it, God struck Egypt, this time with thunder, lightning, and hail that destroyed their crops and livestock. It hailed everywhere except the land of Goshen where the Israelites were located.

In Jeremiah 14:22 and Zechariah 10:1, it is clear who reigns over the rain. In Zechariah 10:1 (KJV), it reads, "Ask ye of the Lord rain in the time of the latter rain; so the Lord shall make bright clouds, and give them showers of rain, to every one grass in the field." Jesus reaffirms this idea in Matthew 5:45 when He says that the Father "makes His sun rise on the evil and on the good, and sends rain on the just and on the unjust." If, after all, Philippians 4:6 counsels us to present our needs to God, why not pray for rain?

It's interesting to note, too, that in I Kings 18:44, after a three-year drought and the elimination of the prophets of Baal on Mount Carmel, the rain clouds move in after being held at bay by Elijah and the power of prayer. Now that's some serious prayer.

When discussing prayer and the weather, I also can't help but remember the time when a friend of mine asked God to clear the fog out of the area so that people could travel safely to work the next day. Normally, when fog settles in, it is due to high moisture content in the air and a lack of wind. That night, while driving home, the fog was dense and there was no wind. The next morning when I went to work there still was no wind but the fog was completely gone. Along those lines I and others have prayed numerous times before destructive storms have moved in only to see the thunderstorm cells split in half or the storms lose their strength.

Giving and Taking via the Wind

One of the other plagues that Egypt experienced during the days of Exodus was that of locusts. Just like the plague of hail, Moses again stretched out his staff over the land of Egypt and this time the Lord sent an east wind that blew all day and night (see Exodus 10:13). By the next morning, that same wind brought swarms of locusts. The result was a complete and thorough stripping of every green plant throughout the land that was not already destroyed by the previous hailstorm. Lest anyone think this was a one-time event, in Revelation 11:6 God empowers two witnesses with the same ability, along with Elijah's ability to stop the rain from falling.

11

In stark contrast, in Numbers 11 we find God using the wind for something else—the delivery of food. At the time there had been complaints by the Israelites in regard to the manna they ate daily. They complained about how the food was better in Egypt, since they had access to fish and vegetables. In Numbers 11:13, Moses then pleads with the Lord, and in verse 31, flocks of quail arrive on the wind. The irony, however, is that it was too much food—so much that the Israelites grew tired of it in a hurry. As the old adage goes, be careful what you ask for.

It's amazing to think that after having the Red Sea parted before them and seeing so many signs of God's existence that they still struggled to believe that God truly had a plan for them and that He could sustain them. In all, waters are parted four times in the Bible: at the Red Sea crossing, when the Israelites crossed the Jordan to enter the Promised Land (see Joshua 3:1 - 4:18), when Elijah and Elisha crossed the Jordan River together (II Kings 2:7-8), and when Elisha returned alone over the same crossing (II Kings 2:13-14). Even though God showed them who was in control of the elements, they still struggled with the issue of faith.

Despite their faith struggles, often times God would tell the Israelites to erect a monument to help them and their children remember what He had done for them. In a similar way, in the summer of 1877, Assumption Chapel was built in the city of Cold Spring, Minnesota, initially as a place of prayer due to the ongoing grasshopper plague. Eventually, however, the site stood as a memorial (until 1894, and then again in 1952) to honor the miracle and the end of the plague. What, then, became of the Rocky Mountain grasshoppers that caused so much damage and destruction?

For an insect that once caused over $200 million in crop damage and once covered an area of 1,700 by 110 miles, their fate is a prairie mystery. By 1902, however, one thing was certain: the Rocky Mountain grasshopper became extinct.

- 2 -

A View of Heaven

"The heavens declare the glory of God; and the firmament shows His handiwork." - Psalm 19:1

From Heaven to Earth and Back Again

In the previous chapter we discussed examples of God's hand at work in the world via the weather and how He shows Himself to be in control of these elements, all the way down to an individual lightning bolt. It also turns out, though, that there are several instances in the Bible where God also reveals elements of Himself via weather related events, almost as if heaven was connected to the earth for brief moments of time.

One of those types of events can be found in II Kings 2:11, where the prophet Elijah and Elisha walked along together. The time had come for Elijah to turn over his ministry to Elisha, although the event was far more dramatic than what one would see in a modern day church. As they walked, suddenly a "chariot of fire" and "horses of fire" took Elijah up by a whirlwind to heaven. In Hebrew, the word here for whirlwind is bassearah, which means storm or tempest. Elijah already had a great deal of direct interaction with God, as seen on Mount Carmel, for example, and in I Kings 19, when he fled the persecution of Ahab and Jezebel.

In I Kings 19, Elijah fled into the wilderness and came to rest under a broom tree where he asked the Lord to take him home. He then fell asleep but was awakened by an angel who told him to get up and to eat (two times). From there he went to Mount Horeb and hid in

13

cave. The Lord confronted him there and asked him to stand at the entrance to the cave. In verses 11 and 12 it reads (KJV), "And he said, Go forth, and stand upon the mount before the Lord. And, behold, the Lord passed by, and a great and strong wind rent the mountains, and brake in pieces the rocks before the Lord; but the Lord was not in the wind: and after the wind an earthquake; but the Lord was not in the earthquake: And after the earthquake a fire; but the Lord was not in the fire: and after the fire a still small voice." It's interesting to note that despite the wind, the earthquake, and the fire, God chose to spoke to his servant with a "still small voice" that amounted to "what are you doing here?" It was as if God wanted to show Elijah that despite all the worldly fears that He was still in charge.

A similar interaction also occurred in the Book of Job after a series of events where Job found himself without his livestock, his family, and even his home. Three "friends" attempt to counsel him for several chapters on end, but in chapter 38 the story takes a dramatic turn. God spoke directly to Job out of a whirlwind similar in nature to that of Elijah's departure. It's unclear from Scripture what type of whirlwind this represents, but several commentaries seem to indicate it is related to clouds and strong winds. According to Job 1:1, Job lived with his family in the land of Uz. The location of Uz is uncertain, but was likely east and/or south of the Sea of Galilee. Although tornadoes are rare in this part of the world, small whirls of dust are seen from time to time in the desert. Whatever the case, the text seems to indicate something more dramatic than a small cloud of whirling dust.

Many other types of interactions that are just as dramatic also occur in several places throughout the Bible. In the transfiguration scene from Matthew 17, when Jesus, Peter, James, and John climbed a high mountain, Moses and Elijah appeared to them. As if that was not enough, soon a "bright cloud" appeared, followed by a voice out of the cloud which said, "This is my beloved Son, in whom I am well pleased; hear ye him." (Matthew 17:5, KJV) In none of these instances, however, does God physically seem to appear—yet He interacts with people just enough to offer a glimpse of His majesty.

Ezekiel's and John's Vision of Heaven

One of the more dramatic views of heaven can be found in the opening chapter of the Book of Ezekiel, where Ezekiel the prophet first hears from the Lord. The vision here depicts a whirlwind or a "great cloud" and a "fire, infolding itself" (Ezekiel 1:4, KJV). What follows is unusual and difficult to picture: coming from within the fire were four creatures in "the likeness of a man". Each had four wings and four faces (one with a face like a lion, another like a calf, one like a man, and another like an eagle) and above them was God on a throne.

In Revelation 4:5, we are given yet another related picture of heaven. Here there is a throne with twenty-four elders seated around it. The elders are dressed in white with gold crowns on their heads seated around it. Again, there are four beasts (one with a face like a lion, another like a calf, one like a man, and another like an eagle), and John describes thunder and lightning as coming out of the throne. Each of the four beasts has six wings apiece and each is full of eyes, and all four praise the Lord continuously.

Pillars of Cloud and Fire

Why does God so often choose to use thunder, lightning, clouds, and even fire to speak to His people? Curiously enough, the most extended and dramatic examples of this phenomenon appear in the Books of Exodus and Numbers. In Exodus 13:21-22, as the Israelites are fleeing Egypt while being chased by Pharaoh's army, we first read of a pillar of cloud and fire: "And the Lord went before them by day in a pillar of cloud to lead the way, and by night in a pillar of fire to give them light, so as to go by day and night. He did not take away the pillar of cloud by day or the pillar of fire by night from before the people."

This pillar led the way into the wilderness, all the way up to the edge of the Red Sea. Then, it moved behind the Israelites and separated them from the Egyptian army (Exodus 14:19). It shone light on the Israelites but appeared as darkness to the Egyptians.

After this, Moses parted the Red Sea and the Israelites crossed on dry land. The Egyptian army pursued them, but again the pillar divided the two groups and threw the army into confusion (Exodus 14:24). After the Israelites were safely on the other side, the sea closed in on the Egyptian army and drowned them. The pillar then moved ahead of the Israelites again and led them both day and night into the wilderness.

Like many other miraculous events in the Bible, however, alternate theories over the years have sprung up in an attempt to explain away these events. For the pillar of fire and cloud, the range of explanations has included everything from volcanoes to fire tornadoes to the Israelites using a "lighted bowl of pitch mounted on a pole". On the surface, those ideas may sound plausible, until one looks at Exodus 14:24: "Now it came to pass, in the morning watch, that the Lord looked down upon the army of the Egyptians through the pillar of fire and cloud, and He troubled the army of the Egyptians." How does one look down from the pillar of fire or cloud and throw an army into chaos? Second, why would an army be confused by a bowl of burning pitch?

Another verse to consider is Exodus 33:9 (KJV), which reads: "And it came to pass, as Moses entered into the tabernacle, the cloudy pillar descended, and stood at the door of the tabernacle, and the Lord talked with Moses." How does a volcanic cloud stand at the door of a tabernacle? To put it another way, how does a fire tornado move in front of the tabernacle without incinerating Moses or the tabernacle cloth itself? Exodus 40:34-38 also indicates that this was a moving cloud that the entire encampment could see. It is also clear from Scripture that this is a cloud moved by intelligence rather than local wind conditions and it went on for *years*.

Along these lines, there is another intriguing occurrence in the Old Testament that is described as the "glory of the Lord". Similar to the pillar of cloud and fire, it hovered over the Tabernacle as a cloud by day and as a fire by night (Numbers 9:15-23). It other instances, it manifested as a cloud after the travelling Tabernacle was built (Exodus 36:9 - 40:33). In Exodus 40:34-38, the cloud filled the tabernacle. While it was there, Moses could not enter.

In I Kings 8:10-12, the cloud filled Solomon's temple. In another instance, the cloud filled the temple after several musicians played instruments and praised the Lord in song (II Chronicles 5:13-14). After the temple was filled, however, the priests could not enter into the areas where the cloud was until it moved to another location. Even in the yet-to-be-built temple described in the Book of Ezekiel (Ezekiel 40-46) the glory of the Lord arrives in a similar, sudden manner

(Ezekiel 43:4-5). The glory of God also illuminates a temple in John's vision in Revelation 21:23.

On Mount Sinai, however, Moses was able to enter the cloud (Exodus 24:15-18) and remained up there for forty days and forty nights. Here, of course, is where God gave Moses the Ten Commandments along with instructions on how to build the Tabernacle.

Future Clouds

The cloud references do not end there, however. Numerous times Jesus' appearance is connected with clouds, and in a more indirect way, lightning and snow. The most prominent example is in Matthew 17, where the Transfiguration occurs. In verse two (KJV), Jesus' "face did shine as the sun, and his raiment was white as the light." Likewise, a similar description can be found in Daniel 7:9: "His garment was white as snow, and the hair of His head was like pure wool. His throne was a fiery flame, its wheels a burning fire." Revelation 1:14 offers a similar description, adding that his eyes were like a "flame of fire". Here, too, John describes His voice as "the sound of many waters" (verse 15).

These verses also echo what is found in Revelation 6:11, where those slain for the Word of God in ages past are told to wait a little longer and are given white robes. The white robes imagery can also be found in Revelation 7:9 (KJV), which reads: "After this I beheld, and, lo, a great multitude, which no man could number, of all nations, and kindreds, and people, and tongues, stood before the throne, and before the Lamb, clothed with white robes, and palms in their hands..." These robes also tie together with Isaiah 1:18 (KJV), "Come now, and let us reason together, saith the LORD: though your sins be as scarlet, they shall be as white as snow; though they be red like crimson, they shall be as wool."

In Acts 1:9, Jesus departed from the presence of His disciples in a curious way: He ascended into heaven and then a cloud hid Him from their sight. Then, as they continued to stare at the sky, two men dressed in white stood beside them and proceeded to tell them that Jesus would return in a likewise manner. Other verses (Matthew 24:30, Revelation 1:7) reinforce this future event, but what is intriguing is that in Revelation 1:7 we are told that "every eye shall see him" (KJV) including "they also which pierced Him". The phrase "they also which pierced Him" refers back to the crucifixion, of course, but the "every eye" phrase makes one think of television (or the internet) and it's ability to reach across the globe in a matter of seconds. It's not clear, however, if that is what is meant or if by some supernatural event everybody will see for themselves His return— even those in regions without any television or only limited forms of communication.

There is one other unusual "lightning" detail which Jesus references in Luke 10:18. Here, Jesus speaks with seventy disciples that were sent out into various towns to preach the Good News. They came back with joy and described the things they had seen and how even demons were subject to them. Jesus tells them "And he said unto them, I beheld Satan as lightning fall from heaven." (KJV) It's not certain at what point in history this event occurred, but perhaps it is tied to Isaiah 14:14, where God describes Satan as wanting to exalt his "throne above the stars of God" and "ascend above the heights of the clouds" to "be like the Most High" (KJV). Instead, of course, he was brought down "to the pit".

- 3 -

The Nature of God

"He has made everything beautiful in its time. Also He has put eternity in their hearts, except that no one can find out the work that God does from beginning to end." - Ecclesiastes 3:11

For as often as the Bible talks about God controlling and interacting with the weather, it also frequently makes comparisons between the supernatural and the weather. Often these comparisons help to bridge our understanding about God's character, the mysteries of the Holy Spirit, and End Times related events. Some of these comparisons are straightforward while others remain mysterious. In some cases, the comparisons are ominous.

The Voice of the Lord

For starters, let's look at what the Word says about God's voice. Probably the most insightful set of verses comes from Psalm 29, where it is described as being like thunder, powerful, full of majesty, "breaks the cedars" (verse 7), and "shakes the wilderness" (verse 8). Joel 3:16 talks about how the Lord will "roar from Zion" and "thunder from Jerusalem" and Jeremiah 25:30 uses similar language. In John 12:28-29, when Jesus spoke briefly to the Father, and the Father replied, some of the bystanders thought they heard thunder.

In other places, the voice of the Lord is described as being like "rushing waters" or "many waters" (Ezekiel 43:2 and Revelation 14:2). If you've ever sat and listened to the sound of a roaring waterfall or even a large set of rapids on a river it may give some hint as to what this voice would sound like. Remember, too, though that back in I Kings 18 God spoke to Elijah not in the wind, the fire, or an earthquake. Instead, He used a still, small voice.

There's more to the voice, however, that just sound waves or the moving of air. Recall back in Genesis 1 this same voice spoke the whole of creation into existence. In Revelation 19:15 it states, "Now out of His mouth goes a sharp sword, that with it He should strike the nations." The sword here is the Word of God, but like the act of creation, it has the power to both create and destroy. In other places the voice of God is conversational, such as with Adam and Eve in the garden, Moses on Mount Sinai, Isaiah's commission (Isaiah 6:8), or Samuel's calling (I Samuel 3:1-21).

The Breath of Life

In many places in Scripture, the Spirit of God is equated with the word breath or breathing. As early as Genesis 2:7 (KJV) we are told, "And the Lord God formed man of the dust of the ground, and breathed into his nostrils the breath of life; and man became a living soul." In Psalm 33:6 (KJV), there is a similar comparison: "By the word of the Lord were the heavens made; and all the host of them by the breath of his mouth."

Not only can the breath of the Lord raise a single person to life but it can also lift up an entire nation as seen in Ezekiel 37 with the nation of Israel. Here, in a vision, God asks Ezekiel to look upon a valley full of dry bones and asks him if He can make them live. God then tells Ezekiel to prophesy to the bones and in the vision not only are the skeletons resurrected, but they are covered with sinews, flesh, and skin (verse 8). In verses nine and ten we read, "Then said he unto me, 'Prophesy unto the wind, prophesy, son of man, and say to the wind, Thus saith the Lord God; Come from the four winds, O breath, and breathe upon these slain, that they may live.' So I prophesied as he commanded me, and the breath came into them, and they lived, and stood up upon their feet, an exceeding great army." An entire army (nation) raised up with just a few words is amazing, and many scholars have linked this vision with the establishment of Israel as a nation in 1948.

Along with breath, the Holy Spirit is also often compared to a unique meteorological element—the wind. In John 3, Jesus tells an inquiring Nicodemus about the need to be born again (via the Holy Spirit) but also makes this comment in verse eight: "The wind blows where it wishes, and you hear the sound of it, but cannot tell where it comes from and where it goes. So is everyone who is born of the Spirit." The wind, of course, is an invisible element in nature, although we can see trees, dust, clouds, and other things move about because of it. As Rev. Billy Graham once quipped, "Have you ever seen the wind? I've seen the effects of the wind but I've never seen the wind. There's a mystery to it."

One of the more famous and dramatic scenes in the New Testament can be found in Acts 2, when the Holy Spirit comes upon a gathering of disciples on the Feast of Pentecost. The topic of Pentecost is deep in its own right, but it was hinted at earlier in John 20:22, where Jesus breathed on His disciples to give them the Holy Spirit. At Pentecost, the Holy Spirit came upon them suddenly, like a "rushing mighty wind" and tongues of fire appeared above them. They then began to speak in tongues, which confounded those gathered outside who heard them speaking in their own native languages. This was the opposite of the event that occurred at the Tower of Babel, where God scattered the builders by giving them different languages to speak.

Chasing the Wind

For all the comparisons between God's spirit and wind, in contrast we are told in the Book of Ecclesiastes *not* to chase after the wind itself. Here, however, "chasing the wind" is compared to a multitude of activities that, by themselves alone, leave life essentially meaningless. The list includes, but is not limited to, work, study, the pursuit of pleasure, and the pursuit of building up wealth for oneself (only to have someone else take it away in the end).

Like the Book of Job, though, initially the Book of Ecclesiastes seems depressing, if not hopeless, until you get to the ending chapter. In Job's situation, his life is restored to double what it was before, and in Ecclesiastes, the main point comes in chapter 12, verse 13, where it reads, "Let us hear the conclusion of the whole matter: Fear God, and keep his commandments: for this is the whole duty of man." (KJV) In other words, without God, life is meaningless. To put it another way, put God first, not the idols of fame, fortune, or popularity, and meaning will fall into place.

Signs of the Times

In the previous chapter, I mentioned how Jesus' appearance during the transfiguration was compared to lightning, and in other instances his clothing was "white as snow". Some intriguing connections develop, however, when you compare these verses with those related to His second coming. In Luke 17:24, Jesus tells us, "For as the lightning that flashes out of one part under heaven shines to the other part under heaven, so also the Son of Man will be in His day." A single lightning bolt, as previously mentioned, can reach over five miles in length and in some cases the return stroke can travel over 60,000 miles per hour!

Along with this event, the End Times have their share of comparisons to the elements of weather, and one of the more sobering passages comes in Matthew 16:1-4. Here, the Pharisees and Sadducees demanded a sign from Jesus as a means of testing Him and His authority. His reply? "'When it is evening you say, 'It will be fair weather, for the sky is red'; and in the morning, 'It will be foul weather today, for the sky is red and threatening.' Hypocrites! You know how to discern the face of the sky, but you cannot discern the signs of the times. A wicked and adulterous generation seeks after a sign, and no sign shall be given to it except the sign of the prophet Jonah.' And He left them and departed." (Matthew 16:2-4)

There are two references in play here. First, Jesus refers to a common saying at the time. A modern day variation is "red sky at night, sailor's delight, red sky at morning, sailors take warning." Second, Jesus referred back to Jonah, an Old Testament prophet who spent three days and three nights inside the belly of a "great fish". The Jonah reference is explained more in Matthew 12:38-42 where Jesus compares Jonah's time in the great fish as a comparison to the time He must spend in the "heart of the earth". In retrospect, this reference was to His crucifixion and resurrection. At the time, though, the Pharisees were oblivious. Oddly enough, Jonah was thrown overboard during a storm at sea.

In Matthew 24, Jesus gives many indications of what the End Times will look like, and although we do not know the exact day or hour of His return, we are told in so many words that we will know the season. Similarly, in Daniel 9:26 we are told, "The end of it shall be with a flood, and till the end of the war desolations are determined."

The flood imagery is further reinforced in Matthew 7:24-27, where Jesus shares a parable about wise and foolish builders. The wise heeded His words and thus built their house (life) on the rock (Himself) but the foolish ignored His words and built their house on sand. When the rain, floods, and wind came, however, the house built by the wise builder stood while the one built by the foolish builder collapsed. One can only imagine the type of "flood" that will occur in the End as many realize they have built their homes (lives) on nothing more than sand. It's interesting that God chose to use such flood imagery in light of the fact that He said back in Genesis that never again would flood *waters* inundate the entire earth.

Then there is the mysterious set of verses in Revelation chapter ten. In Revelation 10:2-3, there is a mighty angel who cries out in a loud voice. John then compares the voice to that of a lion. This is followed in verse four by these cryptic words: "And when the seven thunders had uttered their voices, I was about to write: and I heard a voice from heaven saying unto me, 'Seal up those things which the seven thunders uttered, and write them not.'" (KJV) In other parts of the Book of Revelation, we have the seven seals, seven trumpets, and seven bowls as a means of judgment. These seven thunders occur after the seven seals are opened, and after six of the seven trumpets have sounded. Obviously John did not write these "thunders" down, but it shows that despite all the extensive detail in Revelation and elsewhere on the End of Days, God still has a surprise or two (or seven) up His proverbial sleeve.

The voice of God. The breath of life. The wind of the Holy Spirit. The seven thunders. To some extent, all these examples have to do with the movement of air. More important, though, is that in these first three chapters the emphasis has been on things that are immediate. What about the future, though? Has God ever given a weather forecast in the Bible?

- 4 -

A Long Range Forecast

"To every thing there is a season, and a time to every purpose under the heaven..." - Ecclesiastes 3:1

Over the years, meteorologists have gotten quite a bit of grief over their weather forecasts. After all, who has not been surprised by a storm on their picnic or been warned of a huge snowstorm, only to have most of the snow fall a hundred miles away instead. Behind the scenes, however, weather prediction has improved over the years and many times the public does not realize the calculations, maps, and data that get pored over on a routine basis in an attempt to produce an accurate forecast. These techniques have improved with the advent of better radar and computer models which attempt to forecast weather patterns based on immense sets of data and variables.

Years ago, I had the chance to visit the local weather service office during a day when it was opened up to the public. A brief tour was given by an employee and one of the things they mentioned was the capacity of the banks of machines against the wall that calculated the computer models. They stated that the machines used a great deal of power and that the backup power system for the facility could power a small city for a week. Although the machines and the sophistication of the calculations were impressive, it still fell short of the ultimate weather forecaster: God.

During Joseph's time in Egypt, we get a glimpse of this type of long range forecast. In Genesis 39, Joseph, one of Jacob's sons, was taken down to Egypt as a slave and came to live with Potiphar, an officer of Pharaoh. God was with Joseph and ended up blessing

Potiphar's house. Joseph rose in stature, but one day Potiphar's wife attempted to seduce him. Joseph refused and Potiphar's wife then turned on him. When Potiphar found out, he had Joseph thrown into prison.

Not long after that, Pharaoh's chief butler and chief baker ended up being thrown into the same prison as Joseph (Genesis 40). A short while later, both the butler and the baker had dreams, which Joseph interpreted for them. Although both dreams dealt with their impending release, the butler ended up forgetting about Joseph and the baker was hung on a tree.

Two years after that, Pharaoh had two unique dreams of his own— one where he saw seven healthy cows standing next to seven gaunt-looking cows on a riverbank. In another dream, he saw seven heads of grain on single stalk being consumed by another stalk with seven heads that were "blighted by the east wind" (see Genesis 41:1-7). Pharaoh consulted with magicians and wise men but none could interpret the dreams for him.

The butler then suddenly remembered Joseph, who was still sitting in prison. Pharaoh sent for him and Joseph explained the dreams as being warnings about the future. Indeed, God was going to give Egypt seven years of plenty, followed by seven years of famine. The urgent priority was then to stock up food during the seven good years to help ride out the seven bad ones. Joseph was then elevated to a position of authority over the country. When the famine came, multitudes from other neighboring countries came in search of food, including his own brothers who sold him into slavery.

It is not evident from the text all the factors that led to the famine, although in the crop dream that Pharaoh had, the seven poor heads of grain were withered and blighted by the "east wind". Joseph also stated that the famine would be an act of God (Genesis 41:25-32). A typical famine usually involves crop failures, overpopulation, or even poor government policies. It's possible there was flooding by the Nile River (which was common at the time) or a severe lack of rainfall. Whatever the case, Joseph's stature changed dramatically and the rest of his family eventually moved to Egypt, too.

Future Warnings, Past Parallels

In Revelation 11, we meet two characters whom God will use in multiple ways. These "two witnesses" will be characterized as having a ministry that lasts 1,260 days (or 3 1/2 years) and has many striking parallels to the lives of Elijah and Moses, albeit in a compressed manner in terms of time. They come onto the scene during the End Times tribulation. In Revelation 11:6 (KJV) it reads, "These have power to shut heaven, that it rain not in the days of their prophecy: and have power over waters to turn them to blood, and to smite the earth with all plagues, as often as they will." The plagues echo Moses' time in Egypt and the ability to stop the rain parallels what Elijah did by prayer.

The drama will not stop there, however, for in verse seven it states that the "the beast that ascendeth out of the bottomless pit shall make war against them, and shall overcome them, and kill them." (Revelation 11:7, KJV) For three and a half days their bodies will lay in the streets, and people will *rejoice* over their deaths and exchange gifts with one another. Then God will breathe life back into them and call them towards heaven. Like Jesus' ascension in the Book of Acts, they, too, will ascend towards heaven in a cloud (Revelation 11:42).

What exactly are the plagues they will be able to smite the earth with? From Exodus chapter seven through eleven we see they may involve blood (i.e. waterways turning to blood), frogs, lice (or gnats), flies, livestock disease, boils, hail, locusts, darkness, and the striking down of the firstborn. It will not matter, however, if all of these plagues are unloaded on the earth yet again because people will rejoice when these two prophets are taken out.

Along with the two witnesses there will be multiple other weather-related events that occur near and during the End Times. Although Jesus will return on the clouds, there are some other curious verses in Zechariah, Isaiah, and Revelation that make one wonder if the planet will stop rotating altogether. These End Times weather events will be covered in full in Chapter Eight.

Are past or future prophetic warnings enough, though? Since the day or the hour of Christ's return is unknown, many of these passages can seem distant to some. What about the here and now? Does God currently use weather events to get our attention?

- 5 -

Weather as a Warning

"Thy word is a lamp unto my feet, and a light unto my path." - Psalm 119:105 (KJV)

In August 2009, I was leading a Bible study at a local church based on Ravi Zacharias' video series, "Deliver Us From Evil". The thirteen part series went into great depth about ongoing trends in culture, the church, and with the way the Word is being interpreted by those entrusted to its delivery. Although the study was created over a decade before, it was more relevant than ever.

During week three of the study, we were on lesson number three, which dealt with the Word of God and how some churches and leaders were beginning to interpret Scripture through the lens of the world, rather than letting themselves become transformed by the Word. The study had already proven to be a bit dramatic as news events going on at the time seemed to dovetail with the content of the lessons.

At the same time, a pivotal moment had arrived for the Evangelical Lutheran Church of America, which that church was part of at the time. That week, on Wednesday, August 19th, a debate began on a task force's report on human sexuality at the church's biennial conference. The conference took place that year at the Minneapolis Convention Center in Minneapolis, Minnesota. Leading up to the event, there had been many heated arguments as to the report's meaning and what it meant for individual congregations. There also was a 48-hour round-the-clock prayer vigil held by members of a local church.

One of the other key issues was whether or not the church should repeal the ban on homosexuals in the clergy. Several commentators noted at the time, however, that the real issue was far more profound: how was the Word of God to be interpreted on such issues? Was it relevant anymore on these topics given the direction of the culture in America itself? That Friday, a vote was to be held by the attending delegates on whether to repeal the ban.

On the day of the debate, I was at my day job in an office. The forecast that day was for rain, but there was no mention of thunderstorms. A few minutes before two o'clock in the afternoon, I heard the tornado sirens going off. One glance at the sky gave no indication that a tornado was forming in the clouds or that one was on the way. In bewilderment, I checked the news and found out that a tornado was sighted moving through South Minneapolis. Later that day as I drove home, I noticed the clouds were low and oddly-shaped. After checking the news again, I found out that a tornado tore through South Minneapolis and lifted just as it arrived at the Convention Center in downtown—minutes before the debate, which was scheduled at 2 o'clock. There were multiple other tornado sightings in the region, but this particular one seemed peculiar.

Days later, I happened to look over the National Weather Service's analysis of the event. Sure enough, the environment was not overly conducive to severe weather, and the track of the tornado that traveled through South Minneapolis ended just at the Convention Center, after having travelled straight north (if not even a slightly to the northwest near the latter part of the track) for several miles. Damaged, too, was the church across the street from the center, whose ninety-year old steeple was toppled, leaving the cross dangling upside down. Was this just a coincidence that the debate was about to commence right as the storm hit and ended right where the debate was being held? Or, was God trying to warn the church?

Precedence

In Scripture, there are several examples of where God tried to warn His people directly through weather-related events. The first example comes from Haggai 2:17 where the Lord tells the Israelites, "'I struck you with blight and mildew and hail in all the labors of your hands;

yet you did not turn to Me,' says the Lord." Here, crops were being affected due to lack of repentance, and even after the discipline, apparently there still was no change of heart. In a similar way in Haggai 1:11-12 God criticizes the Israelites for their selfishness and lack of focus on Him by saying, "Therefore the heavens above you withhold the dew, and the earth withholds its fruit. For I called for a drought on the land and the mountains, on the grain and the new wine and the oil, on whatever the ground brings forth, on men and livestock, and on all the labor of your hands."

Now, it might be easy to say that these particular verses were meant for Old Testament times and do not apply to the Christian church, but there is a problem with that point of view, too. As we will see later in this chapter, there are occasions in the future when God will use the exact same means as a method of warning, and in a coming chapter, as a means of judgment. So was God warning the Convention Center meeting attendees of the future to come?

An interesting verse came up in discussion shortly after this event, and it was a verse I had just reread a couple weeks before in my regular, private Bible study time. It was Jeremiah 30:23 (KJV), which reads, "Behold, the whirlwind of the Lord goeth forth with fury, a continuing whirlwind: it shall fall with pain upon the head of the wicked." For some reason I never saw that as a potential "tornado" verse until then and perhaps there was an eerie resonance with the events of that day. Again, whether this particular event was truly a sign or a warning from God is something only God knows for certain, but the conjunction of studies, weather, and the nature of the vote itself does give us something to think about.

Selective Rain

There is also another familiar pattern that God uses when trying to warn or cause repentance. The most well-known illustration is again found in I Kings 8:35-36, during the dedication of the Lord's temple by Solomon, where we can see the potential for rain being withheld due to persistent sin: "When heaven is shut up, and there is no rain, because they have sinned against thee; if they pray toward this place, and confess thy name, and turn from their sin, when thou afflictest them: Then hear thou in heaven, and forgive the sin of thy servants, and of thy people Israel, that thou teach them the good way wherein they should walk, and give rain upon thy land, which thou hast given to thy people for an inheritance." (I Kings 8:35-36, KJV)

The same idea is reinforced in I Kings 17, where Elijah the prophet tells King Ahab that it will only rain upon his command over the next few years (it came to three years total). In Amos 4:7-8, we get more insight when God tells the Israelites: "'I also withheld rain from you, when there were still three months to the harvest. I made it rain on one city, I withheld rain from another city. One part was rained upon, and where it did not rain the part withered. So two or three cities wandered to another city to drink water, but they were not satisfied; yet you have not returned to Me,' says the Lord." In subsequent verses, God tells them He struck their gardens with blight and mildew, their fruit trees with locusts, and even sent upon them some of the plagues that hit Egypt centuries earlier. In other words, it was not as if judgment was going to come without any warnings first.

In the Book of Nahum, which details the decisive judgment of Nineveh (after the warning sent by the prophet Jonah), we see yet another reinforcement of the pattern of warning first, then judgment. In Nahum 1:3 (KJV), it reads: "The Lord is slow to anger and great in power; the Lord will not leave the guilty unpunished. His way is in the whirlwind and the storm, and clouds are the dust of his feet." Nineveh was the capital of the Assyrian Empire and was located on the Tigris River in northeastern Mesopotamia (modern day northern Iraq). It was overthrown by the Medes and the Chaldeans in 612 B.C. and today it stands in ruins.

In addition, Jesus also tells us in Matthew 5:45 that the sun rises on both the good and the evil, and that God sends rain on both the righteous and the unrighteous. Does this verse then negate the other verses I just mentioned? No, because the sun shines on the entire planet and rain also falls in many places. The point here, though, is that God can use instances of weather, even over the long term, to address sin issues of a people before long judgment falls.

Future Warnings

So far, most of the examples I've presented in this chapter have involved the Israelites and God's past dealings with them. It may be tempting at this point to think that the era of using weather to warn has long since passed. Yet in Exodus 9:29 (KJV), Moses told Pharaoh, "As soon as I am gone out of the city, I will spread abroad my hands unto the Lord; and the thunder shall cease, neither shall there be any more hail; that thou mayest know how that the earth is the Lord's." Whether then, now, or in the future, here and in multiple other locations in Scripture it is clear that God is in charge of the entire planet.

Looking to the future, however, as I mentioned in a previous chapter, God will send two witnesses (Revelation 11) who will preach, be able to strike the earth with any of a number of plagues, and stop the rain falling as necessary. If that were not dramatic enough, in the Millennial Kingdom era, entire nations may experience drought conditions due to a lack of worship for the Messiah, who will rule and reign from Jerusalem (Zechariah 14:17). In the next verse, Egypt is singled out as having the same condition, with the added provision that "they shall receive the plague with which the Lord strikes the nations who do not come up to keep the Feast of Tabernacles." Although the study of the Millennial Kingdom is worth an entire book on its own, it's interesting to see a return of a few of the feast days, along with some climate changes which will be covered in a later chapter.

So where does that leave us now? Are we in some sort of "in between" age where God has used weather in the past and will do so again in the future? In a couple of chapters, I'll cover New Testament examples of how and why warning and judgment can still occur in this present age.

- 6 -

Weather as a Weapon

"The horse is prepared for the day of battle, but deliverance is of the Lord." - Proverbs 21:31

In the summer of 1814, the United States was in the middle of the War of 1812 with the British Empire. On August 24, 1814, British warships sailed up the Patuxent River and anchored in Maryland. A few thousand British soldiers then disembarked and marched towards the city of Washington in hopes of capturing the city in retaliation for the burning of the British capital in Canada. The American forces gathered there clashed with the British forces but soon the American forces were routed. Residents of the city fled, and by nightfall, an order was given to set fire to the city.

By the next morning the city was still burning, and British soldiers continued to set fire to buildings and destroyed parts of the city. In the afternoon, however, a storm rolled in and with it came a tornado. The twister destroyed more buildings and made a direct hit on the British occupation forces, and damaged numerous artillery pieces. Several soldiers were killed, and when the British forces eventually left that evening, their return trek was hindered by downed trees. They returned to their ships but found damaged riggings. A couple of the ships had even broken free from where they were anchored. The forces never returned.

Is it possible that God intervened in this instance?

In World War II, another unique weather-related event occurred between May 26 and June 3, 1940. Later to be called the "Miracle of Dunkirk" and a "miracle of deliverance" by Winston Churchill, it involved the rescue of over 300,000 Allied troops from the German forces in and around the beaches of Dunkirk, France. King George VI of the United Kingdom had already called for a day of prayer on May 26, due to the dire situation of the Allied forces. Fog and clouds eventually enveloped the region, and the English Channel remained calm while many "little ships" (private fishing boats, cruisers, and some commercial vessels) shuttled soldiers from the beaches to nearby destroyers. The weather pattern held during the entire evacuation until the beaches were emptied.

There are many more examples like these listed here, but the question remains: has God intervened in the past in times of war in order to turn the tide of battle? We've already established that local weather and climate as a whole is under God's ultimate control, and in the last chapter I mentioned how God can use the weather as a way to call for repentance. What if the tide of battle changed by simply stopping troops or equipment in their tracks with floods, winds, or storms?

In the battle-themed Psalm 144, David pleads with the Lord concerning his enemies and asks, "Cast forth lightning, and scatter them: shoot out thine arrows, and destroy them." (KJV, verse 6). When David was delivered from the hand of Saul in the second book of Samuel, he praised God by saying, "The Lord thundered from heaven, and the Most High uttered His voice. He sent out arrows and scattered them; lightning bolts, and He vanquished them." (II Samuel 22:14-15) Were these just colorful descriptions or are there other places where God has turned the tide of battle in Scripture?

One of the more prominent examples of God altering a battle can be found in Joshua 10, where not only did the sun stand still for nearly a day (verses 1-15), but God rained hailstones on the Amorite kings and their troops as they fled the Israelites. According to verse 11, more troops died because of the hailstones than by the swords of the Israelites. This incident brings up several intriguing points: not only did hail take out troops, but in order for the sun to stand still, it would imply that potentially the Earth stopped rotating for part of a day. There has been a great deal of conjecture as to the astronomical events on that day (such as sudden changes in the orbits of Earth and Mars), but it was not the first time that a battle was influenced by God.

In Exodus 14:19-20, we read about how an angel of the Lord moved from the front of Israel's army to travel behind them. At the same time, the pillar of cloud moved there, also, and came between their army and the Egyptian troops. In addition, the cloud brought darkness to one side and light to the other, effectively putting up a wall between the two groups. In I Samuel 7:10, we read about how the prophet Samuel was offering a burnt offering to the Lord, and suddenly the Philistines attempted to attack. The result? "But the Lord thundered with a loud thunder upon the Philistines that day, and so confused them that they were overcome before Israel."

Future Weapons

There are two wars listed in Old Testament prophecy that have yet to occur, but show that God will exercise His control over the elements yet again in times of battle. The first war, which some commentators have noted may immediately precede the second, larger war, occurs in Psalm 83. It is difficult to connect the participants in this particular battle with any historical event, which makes it unique among the Psalms.

Here, a confederacy of nations ringing Israel gathers together and attacks. The list includes Edom and Ishmaelites (Southern Jordan, Saudi Arabia), Moab (central Jordan), the Hagrites (Egypt), Gebal (northern Lebanon), Ammon (northern Jordan), Amalek (region south of Israel), Philistia (Gaza strip), Tyre (southern Lebanon) and Assyria (Syria and parts of Iraq). In verse four, these nations declare, "Come, and let us cut them off from being a nation; that the name of Israel may be no more in remembrance." (KJV) The psalm is ascribed to Asaph, who was a leader of one of David's Levitical choirs, and in verses 14 and 15 he declares, "As the fire burneth a wood, and as the flame setteth the mountains on fire; So persecute them with thy tempest, and make them afraid with thy storm." (KJV)

Compared to a modern day map of the Middle East, the lineup of nations in this Psalm refers to regions that are currently becoming increasingly hostile towards the nation of Israel. Some scholars have noted that the outcome of this particular war could draw in larger nations, and possibly those listed in the Gog-Magog War of Ezekiel 38 and 39. Whatever the outcome, this is not the first time in Scripture where a nation (or nations) attempt to take out Israel, nor will it be the last.

The larger Gog-Magog War, found in Ezekiel 38 and 39, contains vivid details in its own right. The list of nations for that war looks like this: Persia (Iran), Cush (parts of Sudan), Put (Libya), Gomer (southwestern Turkey), Beth Togarmah (eastern Turkey), Meshech (northeastern Turkey), Tubal (northwestern Turkey), and Magog (Russia?). Although there is a great deal of debate on the exact modern-day locations of these names, again, this is yet another battle that will involve nations working together to destroy the nation of Israel. This time, however, the players are much bigger, and the cleanup will be so extensive it will take seven months to complete the work (see Ezekiel 39:12-16).

Despite the all-out attack by multiple nations, God will pour out judgment on the participants and the leader that orchestrates it all (Gog). God "will plead against him (Gog) with pestilence and with blood; and I will rain upon him, and upon his bands, and upon the many people that are with him, an overflowing rain, and great hailstones, fire, and brimstone. Thus will I magnify myself, and sanctify myself; and I will be known in the eyes of many nations, and they shall know that I am the Lord." (Ezekiel 38:22-23, KJV) The carnage will be so vast that Israel will be able to burn up the abandoned weapons for fuel for seven years (Ezekiel 39:9).

In both wars, however, it seems that some form of storm, tempest, and/or hailstones will be used. Although we cannot know for certain when these battles will take place, one look at the current news headlines seems to indicate one or both of these may be just around the corner on the prophetic timeline.

- 7 -

Weather as Judgment

"I set My rainbow in the cloud, and it shall be for the sign of the covenant between Me and the earth. It shall be, when I bring a cloud over the earth, that the rainbow shall be seen in the cloud; and I will remember My covenant which is between Me and you and every living creature of all flesh; the waters shall never again become a flood to destroy all flesh." - Genesis 9:13-15

On August 17, 2005, a major event in Gaza had many in an uproar. President George Bush and Secretary of State Condoleezza Rice had encouraged Israeli Prime Minister Ariel Sharon to forcibly evacuate over 9,000 residents from the Gaza Strip, leaving many of the residents homeless at first. Pressure had been applied for years by the U.S. Government and others with the hopes of eventually creating a "two-state" solution in the region as a means of bringing peace between Israel and surrounding peoples. The evacuation ended on August 22.

On August 23, tropical depression twelve formed over the Southeastern Bahamas. By the following day, it was upgraded to a tropical storm and given the name "Katrina". A day after that, it was upgraded to a minimal hurricane before it made landfall in Florida. The storm then moved back out over open water and intensified rapidly in the Gulf of Mexico, and within days it reached category five strength on the Saffir-Simpson Hurricane Scale. Winds topped out at a fierce 175 miles per hour, before dropping back down a bit. On August 29, the hurricane smashed into the Louisiana and Mississippi coastlines causing catastrophic damage. In the end, at least 1,800 lives were lost, thousands were left homeless, and the storm became the costliest hurricane in American history with an estimated property damage total of $108 billion.

Numerous rabbis, Christian leaders, and commentators at the time drew connections between the events. The parallels were eerie, including residents of New Orleans climbing on their rooftops to escape the rising floodwaters and Gaza residents climbing on *their* rooftops to escape the evacuation orders. Katrina destroyed thousands of homes and buildings and Israel military bulldozers leveled many structures in Gaza. Dead bodies floated in the floodwaters of New Orleans and in Gaza, several bodies were dug up from local cemeteries. Another angle that many commentators pointed out was that New Orleans had become a hub for occult activity. Was God judging America for its stance with Israel? Did He send an epic storm in order to send a message to the entire nation?

Does Judgment Still Happen?

Let's back up a minute. Implicit in these discussions is that God is still in the business of judging individuals and even entire nations. The usual Biblical correction pattern is that God will send warnings first as a means of correction and getting one's attention. Then, if sin persists, a certain threshold seems to be reached and judgment occurs. This judgment may involve death, destruction, disease, invading armies, or supernatural events. Yet does this pattern apply to modern-day Christians who believe that Jesus' perfect sacrifice covers all their sins?

In I Corinthians 11:27-32, Paul warns that if someone takes the blood and wine commemorating Jesus' work at the cross in an unworthy manner, they run the risk of becoming weak, sick, or even dying (verse 29) because they are drinking judgment on themselves. In this case, it is an act of discipline, but the consequences can be dire. Hebrews 12:1-12 also speaks of God disciplining His children, but does not get into specifics of how this is accomplished. Revelation 3:19 also talks of how discipline can occur in the context of love even for an entire church.

In Acts 4:32-37, we get a glimpse of the early church, with believers fully sharing their possessions with one another. In contrast, in Acts 5:1-11, we learn of Ananias and Sapphira, who sold a piece of property but withheld some of the earnings. They laid down only some of the earnings before the apostles and as a result, Peter confronted Ananias. Peter indicated that Ananias lied to the Holy Spirit and moments later Ananias fell dead. A few hours later, his wife stopped by and was also confronted. The end result was the same.

Despite these verses and others, one also has to be careful not to fall into the trap of attributing every single event as a direct product of sin and subsequent judgment. Not only do we not know the mind of God on the issue of Hurricane Katrina, but in Luke 13:4-5, Jesus addresses the issue of guilt and sin by bringing up a recent event at that time: "Or those eighteen on whom the tower in Siloam fell and killed them, do you think that they were worse sinners than all other men who dwelt in Jerusalem? I tell you, no; but unless you repent you will all likewise perish."

Thousands of people suffered as a result of the storm, regardless of their belief systems, and to this day many families who lived in New Orleans and surrounding communities have never returned. 2005 was also an exceptional year for the Atlantic hurricane season, with a series of intense, destructive storms including Katrina, Rita, Wilma, and even several storms whose names started with Greek letters.

Past Judgments

Scripture is filled with several examples of how weather has been used as a form of judgment and we have already covered some major examples in previous chapters. From the plagues of Exodus to hail raining down on armies, it is clear God can and has been willing in the past to use such measures to pour out judgment or to get His point across.

An interesting chapter to look at when discussing this subject is Hosea chapter eight. Here, God (through the prophet Hosea) confronted Israel on its rebellion. In verse seven it reads, "For they have sown the wind, and they shall reap the whirlwind: it hath no stalk; the bud shall yield no meal: if so be it yield, the strangers shall swallow it up." (KJV) In phrasing reminiscent of Ecclesiastes' "chasing the wind", God showed the Israelites the consequences of their decisions would be dire. In this situation, it was idolatry, and with other nations, including Assyria. Israel at the time looked to an empire like Assyria for protection, but ultimately it led them away from God and in turn God used Assyria to deliver judgment.

Although the word "whirlwind" is the same as was used in II Kings 2:1 when Elijah went up to heaven in a whirlwind, here it seems to be used in a metaphoric sense. It's unclear whether there was any physical destruction due to the weather, although the last half of verse seven implies drought conditions. Even if there was no drought, foreigners would have taken whatever was produced anyway.

Another major example of past judgments God has wrought through the weather is of course the Great Flood in the days of Noah (see Genesis 6-9). There have been many theories as to what the atmosphere may have been like in the days before the Flood, and many scholars seem to think that *something* was different about our planet during those times. For one, there is no clear indication in the chapters preceding Genesis 6 that it ever rained. In Genesis 2:5-6 (KJV), we find that "every plant of the field before it was in the earth, and every herb of the field before it grew: for the Lord God had not caused it to rain upon the earth, and there was not a man to till the ground. But there went up a mist from the earth, and watered the whole face of the ground." When the Flood came, in Genesis 7:11 (KJV) it states, "In the six hundredth year of Noah's life, in the second month, the seventeenth day of the month, the same day were all the fountains of the great deep broken up, and the windows of heaven were opened." If there was no rain before the Flood, it must have made Noah's boatbuilding efforts seem even crazier to the casual observer.

This judgment, at least in this form, was truly a one-time event. We know this fact because God makes a covenant in Genesis 9:13-15 to *not* flood the earth again. Yet in Matthew 24:37-39, Jesus warns that the End Times will parallel the "days of Noah" since the floodwaters came suddenly and took many people away. So too, will His Second Coming catch everyone by surprise.

Future Judgments

The End Times have some dramatic weather events of their own, and in a few situations, it appears those events will be unique not only due to their sheer scale, but also to their strangeness compared to weather nowadays. In Revelation 7:1, just before the 144,000 servants from the tribes of Israel are sealed by God, John sees "four angels standing on the four corners of the earth, holding the four winds of the earth, that the wind should not blow on the earth, nor on the sea, nor on any tree." (KJV) Where in Joshua 10 the sun stood still, here the winds stand still for a moment in time. Without the wind, clouds would stop moving, the air would become stale, and thunderstorms would collapse. Weather systems would come to a standstill and if it went on long enough, drought would set in.

In Revelation 8:7, when the first trumpet sounds, we see "hail and fire mingled with blood, and they were cast upon the earth: and the third part of trees was burnt up, and all green grass was burnt up." (KJV) Hail mixed with fire is quite the contrast visually and meteorologically. The hailstones don't stop there, though. In Revelation 16:21, it talks about hail, too: "And great hail from heaven fell upon men, each hailstone about the weight of a talent. Men blasphemed God because of the plague of the hail, since that plague was exceedingly great." What is the "weight of a talent"? It was probably between 75 and 100 pounds at the time Revelation was written.

Read that again slowly: 100 *pound* hailstones. Hail forms when supercooled raindrops are swept up in a thunderstorm's updraft. Ice then continues to accumulate until the weight of the hailstone overcomes the strength of the updraft. At that point, the hailstone falls out of the cloud. The largest hailstone on record in the United States was about eight inches across and weighed 1.93 pounds. It fell in Vivian, South Dakota in July of 2010. To achieve a 100 pound hailstone, each stone would have to be greater than 20 inches across! To create a four-inch diameter hailstone, it takes winds of nearly 100 mph in the updraft. Gigantic hailstones may then imply freakish atmospheric winds, too.

On a side note, there's a curious term used in certain places in the Bible to describe where the wind and other elements come from: storehouses (or treasuries, depending on the translation you use). It's found in Psalm 135:7, where it reads: "He causes the vapors to ascend from the ends of the earth; He makes lightning for the rain; He brings the wind out of His treasuries." It's also found in Job 38:22-23 where God asks Job, "Have you entered the treasury of snow, or have you seen the treasury of hail, which I have reserved for the time of trouble, for the day of battle and war?"

In Hebrew, the word "storehouse" is otsar, which means a treasury, store, storehouse, or even armory. It's unclear from Scripture, where these are located and whether it refers to thunderheads or the upper atmosphere in general.

These examples are only a sample of some of the wide variety of judgments to come in the End Times. In the next chapter we'll look at some other unusual developments that will truly redefine the popular phrase "climate change".

- 8 -

End Times Climate Change

"There shall be no night there: They need no lamp nor light of the sun, for the Lord God gives them light. And they shall reign forever and ever." - Revelation 22:5

In late November and early December 2010, negotiators from 192 countries met in Cancun, Mexico, for the United Nations climate change summit. Although the goal of a previous summit was to develop a broad international treaty to fight global warming, this meeting was meant to set goals for reducing greenhouse gas emissions and to find ways to set up a fund to help poor countries acquire more environmentally-friendly technology. The meeting opened with Christiana Figueres, executive secretary of the U.N. Framework Convention on Climate Change, invoking the "ancient jaguar goddess Ixchel" in her opening statements. In a strange twist, near the end of the conference, Cancun broke a 100-year old record low with a temperature of 54 degrees.

Although Al Gore was not in attendance at this conference, a few years earlier his documentary, "An Inconvenient Truth", attempted to weave together several pieces of data on climate change which looked intriguing on the surface, but were connected in a tenuous way. The documentary, and subsequent climate change conferences, were meant to start conversation and create legislation in hopes of heading off a potential crisis in the coming decades. The main take home message from the documentary and these conferences is this, however: climate change is our fault.

It is really our fault though? To add to the debate, back in February

2010, Bill Gates, former chairman of Microsoft, gave a Ted Talk that explored the need to reduce carbon dioxide emissions on a global scale. Included in the talk was a formula that looked like this:

$$CO_2 = P \times S \times E \times C$$

...where P = Population, S = Services, E = Efficiency/energy for each service, and C = the amount of CO_2 put out for each unit of energy.

He made two mysterious comments in the speech, however. The first one was that in order to stop global warming, we would need to get the carbon dioxide levels to zero. That means the left side of the equation would be equal to zero. He then went on to explain each factor on the right side of the equation, starting with the letter P. He noted how the world's population will soon climb to nine billion people. Then came this curious statement: "Now if we do a really great job on new vaccines, health care, and reproductive health services we could lower that by perhaps 10 or 15 percent."

Wait. How does improving on vaccines *reduce* population growth? What did he mean by "reproductive health services"? The rest of his speech was spent discussing the other factors of the equation and how we will be unable to get the last factor reduced to zero (especially by using fossil fuels). He also mentioned the need to create a new system on a "global scale" and the need for "energy miracles".

There are some issues with this equation, however. What were the levels of carbon dioxide like in the atmosphere prior to the Industrial Revolution? Have they risen or fallen naturally over the centuries? How have cosmic rays interacted with the atmosphere over the centuries?

Implicit in this equation, and the talk itself, is that we are the ones in control of the planet's temperature and that at some point, things will be pushed into "crisis mode". Will that crisis involve reducing various factors in the equation (including population) in order to turn down the temperature of the planet in order to save people?

Often times when the subject of climate change comes up, the topic of melting polar caps and rising seas comes with it. If the polar caps melt, where will the people go to live? Will they race to the mountains or build large boats if the seas start rising? Will whole island countries be inundated by the oceans and will wars start as a result?

In late 2011, an ominous article appeared in The Independent which cited the discovery of gigantic methane "plumes" on the Arctic sea floor, which were over 1,000 meters across and seeping methane into the ocean. Methane, the article stated, is twenty times more potent than carbon dioxide as a greenhouse gas. Should the Siberian permafrost and the sea ice continue to disappear, huge quantities of methane could be released into the atmosphere, throwing it out of balance on a never-before-seen scale.

Yet in Genesis 9:11, God tells us, "Thus I establish My covenant with you: Never again shall all flesh be cut off by the waters of the flood; never again shall there be a flood to destroy the earth." Will the ice caps melt enough to wipe out whole nations and destroy some (but not all) coastal cities? In Job 38:8-11 God tells Job: "Or who shut in the sea with doors, when it burst forth and issued from the womb; when I made the clouds its garment, and thick darkness its swaddling band; when I fixed My limit for it, and set bars and doors; when I said, 'This far you may come, but no farther, and here your proud waves must stop!'"

So what does the Bible say about global warming and climate change? Although it does not address the issue directly, two future periods on the Earth will bring their own forms of climate change, and they will look nothing like the potential horror stories that bombard us through the media on a daily basis.

A Millennial Forecast

After Christ's return on the clouds (Matthew 24:30) and the tumultuous events of the first nineteen chapters of the Book of Revelation, the Bible talks about a period called the "Millennium" or the Millennial Kingdom, where Christ will reign and rule over the earth from Jerusalem. Numerous verses, both in the Old and the New Testament, point to this unique period in history. This age, along with the post-Millennium period, also have several unique features when it comes to climate and astronomical events.

Starting in Zechariah 14, we can see some of these events. The first five verses describe how the Lord will come to reign from Jerusalem, and how He will come to fight against many nations at once. He will once again stand on the Mount of Olives, but this time there will be a great, mountain-splitting earthquake. Living water will also begin to flow from Jerusalem, to the Dead Sea in one direction and to the Mediterranean in the other. Verses six and seven read, "It shall come to pass in that day that there will be no light; the lights will diminish. It shall be one day which is known to the Lord—neither day nor night. But at evening time it shall happen that it will be light."

Verses twelve through fifteen then talk of a horrific plague that will strike the nations that attacked Israel. Then, in verses sixteen through nineteen we learn that the survivors in those nations (and all peoples of the earth, really) will need to go up to Jerusalem on a yearly basis (centered around the Feast of Tabernacles) or else they will receive no rain. In verse eighteen, Egypt is also singled out and the warning of a lack of rain is reiterated for them.

Fishing the Dead Sea

Connected to the living water flowing to the east and to the west of Jerusalem is the existence of the Millennial temple, which is described in the Book of Ezekiel, chapters 40-48. When the living water flows into the Dead Sea, however, drastic changes will occur.

Nowadays, the Dead Sea is devoid of marine life. Blobs of asphalt bubble up from the bottom and enough salt is in the water to cause virtually anybody to float on top of the waves with no effort. In other words, forget about bringing your fishing rod.

It is approximately 42 miles long, up to eleven miles wide, and 1,237 feet deep at the deepest point. The water has a salt concentration around 31.5%, which means it is over eight times saltier than the world's oceans. On the north end, the Jordan River flows in. On the southeastern shore, it is believed the cities of Sodom and Gomorrah once stood, which were destroyed by fire and brimstone (see Genesis 18 and 19) in an act of judgment. On the eastern shore, there is also the remains of a fortified city (Bab edh-Dhra) that has a seven foot layer of ash...which may later prove to be the real ruins of one of these cities.

David also fled from King Saul to the nearby "wilderness of En-Gedi", which is on the western shore (see I Samuel 24:1-2). Additionally, nearby are the caves of Qumram where the Dead Sea

Scrolls were found. Nowadays, however, the Dead Sea is shrinking in size. It may also look as if this place is in need of a massive toxic cleanup considering all the minerals in the water and along the shoreline.

God, however, has a restoration plan for this area. It starts with the living water flowing into the sea, and in Ezekiel 47:8-12 an amazing landscape is described:

> "Then he said to me: 'This water flows toward the eastern region, goes down into the valley, and enters the sea. When it reaches the sea, its waters are healed. And it shall be that every living thing that moves, wherever the rivers go, will live. There will be a very great multitude of fish, because these waters go there; for they will be healed, and everything will live wherever the river goes. It shall be that fishermen will stand by it from En Gedi to En Eglaim; they will be places for spreading their nets. Their fish will be of the same kinds as the fish of the Great Sea, exceedingly many. But its swamps and marshes will not be healed; they will be given over to salt. Along the bank of the river, on this side and that, will grow all kinds of trees used for food; their leaves will not wither, and their fruit will not fail. They will bear fruit every month, because their water flows from the sanctuary. Their fruit will be for food, and their leaves for medicine.'"

In other words, God will heal this particular region and flood the sea with fish. How, exactly, the salt will be removed is a mystery, but this follows a pattern found elsewhere in the Bible. That pattern is one of the giving of law, followed by lawbreaking, followed by warnings, then judgment, and finally restoration. This same pattern occurred with the nation of Israel with the giving of the Law through Moses, their gradual drifting away from God, warnings from the prophets, followed by exile, and then their restoration to their homeland.

Much like the Dead Sea's future restoration, *anyone* can experience the kind of restoration God can offer. This can be found in II Peter 3:9 where it states, "The Lord is not slack concerning his promise, as some men count slackness; but is longsuffering to us-ward, not willing that any should perish, but that all should come to repentance." (KJV) Like the Samaritan woman in John 4, the offer of "living water" stands for anyone who is willing to receive it. As you can see, if God can restore one of the most lifeless regions on earth, He can restore anything or anyone.

More Oddities

Another oddity of this period (or perhaps of the subsequent New Jerusalem era) will be the strange fulfillment of Isaiah 60:19, which reads, "The sun shall no longer be your light by day, nor for brightness shall the moon give light to you; but the Lord will be to you an everlasting light, and your God your glory." Does this mean that the sun will stop shining? Will the earth stop rotating?

It will also be a time when the "The wolf and the lamb shall feed together, the lion shall eat straw like the ox," (Isaiah 65:25) In some ways this verse may be an echo of Genesis 1:30 (KJV) which states, "And to every beast of the earth, and to every fowl of the air, and to every thing that creepeth upon the earth, wherein there is life, I have given every green herb for meat: and it was so." There has been some speculation over the years that land-based animals were herbivores before the Fall, but whatever the case, it appears there will be peace between different types of wildlife.

Global Warming Overdrive

After the Millennial reign ends, there is a curious period where the Book of Revelation describes Satan being released from captivity to "deceive the nations once more". After this final battle, he is thrown into a lake of fire (Revelation 20:10) to be tormented forever. In Revelation 21:4 (KJV), God tells us He will "wipe away all tears from their eyes; and there shall be no more death, neither sorrow, nor crying, neither shall there be any more pain: for the former things are passed away." If that is not enough, look at what happens next.

In Revelation 21:10-16 (KJV) John writes:

"And he carried me away in the spirit to a great and high mountain, and shewed me that great city, the holy Jerusalem, descending out of heaven from God, Having the glory of God: and her light was like unto a stone most precious, even like a jasper stone, clear as crystal; And had a wall great and high, and had twelve gates, and at the gates twelve angels, and names written thereon, which are the names of the twelve tribes of the children of Israel: On the east three gates; on the north three gates; on the south three gates; and on the west three gates.

And the wall of the city had twelve foundations, and in them the names of the twelve apostles of the Lamb. And he that talked with me had a golden reed to measure the city, and the gates thereof, and the wall thereof. And the city lieth foursquare, and the length is as large as the breadth: and he measured the city with the reed, twelve thousand furlongs. The length and the breadth and the height of it are equal."

Since 12,000 furlongs is roughly equivalent to 1,400-1,500 miles, it appears this passage speaks of a gigantic cube or maybe even a pyramid. Where on earth would you put such a massive structure? Putting the center of it on the site of modern day Jerusalem would mean that part of it would stretch out over the Mediterranean Sea, while the other end would be somewhere in far eastern Iraq. To the north, it would cover parts of Turkey, and to the south it would go into Sudan. Architecturally, that seems a little unrealistic given the current topography of the land in that region of the world.

The answer to this question appears to be found in Revelation 21:1, which talks of a new heaven and a new earth, but more importantly it states there will be "no more sea". Perhaps this verse fits together and illuminates what Peter said in II Peter 3:10 where he wrote, "But the day of the Lord will come as a thief in the night, in which the heavens will pass away with a great noise, and the elements will melt with fervent heat; both the earth and the works that are in it will be burned up."

Now if this event occurs before the New Jerusalem is lowered from the clouds, does that mean that the oceans and seas must be boiled off first? What about the canyons left behind when the seas evaporate? Then again, a 1,400 mile cube coming down from above would probably crush anything in its path.

In the end it seems, global warming really will become a reality, just not in the way most people think.

Reduce, Reuse, Recycle

Do these future events excuse Christians from taking care of the earth since it's all going to be burned up anyway? Hardly. Right after the verse where Peter talks about the heavens disappearing with a roar, he writes these lines (verses 11 and 12), "Therefore, since all these things will be dissolved, what manner of persons ought you to be in holy conduct and godliness, looking for and hastening the coming of the day of God, because of which the heavens will be dissolved, being on fire, and the elements will melt with fervent heat?" (II Peter 3:11-12)

What about carbon dioxide emissions? Should we continue to use fossil fuels indiscriminately since God is in charge of the planet's climate anyway?

No. There is much to be gained by moving away from certain fuels including reduced pollution, less dependence on foreign sources of oil, better use of available natural resources, etc. Additionally, recycling plastic, metal, glass, paper, and other items can be a great way to reuse the earth's resources and lead to new uses of such materials. Many stories can be told of landfills running out of space and some have problems with chemicals leaching into the ground.

Also, as of the writing of this book, there is still a huge island of plastic particles and chemical sludge floating in the Pacific Ocean called the "Great Pacific Garbage Patch". It is roughly located between Japan and California (in terms of latitude) and reports vary as to its size. It is invisible to satellite photography, although tests of the water column in the area show a very high concentration of decomposing plastic particles. The source of all the particles is unknown, although the ocean currents often cause such contaminants to pool together in one location.

Additionally, in Scripture, we are told to be good stewards of what we are given, including the earth and its resources. Psalm 115:16 tells us, "The heaven, even the heavens, are the Lord's: but the earth hath he given to the children of men." (KJV). Psalm 8:6-8 and Genesis 1:26 tell us that man is to rule over the creatures of the earth and all the earth itself. In Exodus 23:10-12, God tells the Israelites that for six years they could work the land, but every seventh year they were supposed to let it rest. The danger comes in turning such things into objects of worship or turning them into idols as a substitute for a relationship with God.

- 9 -

Faith Under Siege

"For I know that my Redeemer lives..." - Job 19:25

Throughout this book, we've discussed what the Bible says about God, the weather, and climate. It's evident that God has ultimate control and sovereignty over all aspects of the weather, and that in the future "global warming" will take on a whole new meaning. Yet what does Scripture say about the storms of life? Who is in control when everything in your life is falling apart around you and it seems you cannot find a safe harbor from the wind and waves?

Faith in the Boat

Three of the four Gospels tell the brief tale of when Jesus got into a boat with His disciples (see Matthew 8:23-27). They set sail on the Sea of Galilee, but once out on the water, Jesus fell asleep. Soon, a violent storm came up and the waves began to drive water into the boat. The disciples panicked and woke Jesus up, telling Him they thought they were going to drown. Jesus then rebuked the wind and the waves and sea suddenly went calm. He also told them, "Why are ye fearful, O ye of little faith?" (Matthew 8:26, KJV). At this point, the disciples were amazed that He could command the sea and the wind. Yet notice His response was not, "That's right. Look what I can do." Instead, He used it as a moment to build their faith when it looked like all hope was lost.

When the storms of life sweep over our individual boats, what do we do? Do we panic like the disciples, forget who God is, and even get angry? In several places the Bible tells us that believers will undergo trials and persecution. In some regions of the world, that persecution can mean prison time, torture, destruction of personal property, and even martyrdom. For others it may be hostility in the workplace, strife within one's family, or the loss of friendships.

Yet what are the common responses to those trials? Some may say, "it's my burden to bear" and others will say "it's the Lord's will". Sometimes others will tell you "you just need to have more faith!" In other instances, gossip will spread because, after all, "there must be some sin you haven't confessed!" Many times those questions and doubts can do a lot more harm than good. Even well meaning friends, family members, and other Christians can say things that are more humiliating than helpful.

What does the Scripture say about these trials? In Matthew 5:11-12, Jesus tells us we will be blessed when are persecuted for His sake. Our reward in heaven will be great, for "so they persecuted the prophets who were before you." In James 1:2-4, we are told that the testing of our faith will produce perseverance, and that will in turn produce maturity and completion. These same verses tell us to consider these trials as "pure joy", although that is easier said than done. Often times, too, it's easy to question whether God sees everything we are going through.

This brings up another point—does God see everything we have to deal with? The answer is, yes, He does see it and He will see us through. How do I know this? Consider these verses:

> **Romans 8:38-39** – "For I am persuaded that neither death nor life, nor angels nor principalities nor powers, nor things present nor things to come, nor height nor depth, nor any other created thing, shall be able to separate us from the love of God which is in Christ Jesus our Lord."

> **Hebrews 13:5** – "For He Himself has said, 'I will never leave you nor forsake you.'"

> **I Samuel 16:7** – When Jesse's sons are lined up before the prophet Samuel, and Samuel has been told by the Lord to anoint a successor to King Saul, the Lord tells him, "For the Lord does

not see as man sees; for man looks at the outward appearance, but the Lord looks at the heart."

II Chronicles 16:9 – "For the eyes of the Lord run to and fro throughout the whole earth, to show Himself strong on behalf of those whose heart is loyal to Him."

There are other verses that reinforce these same ideas (for instance, see Psalm 139), but the main point is this: God does see everything that happens here on Earth. That's either a convicting idea or a liberating one depending on where you stand with Him and what's going on in your life.

Taking it Up in Prayer

Okay, so we know that Christians are going to go through trials. We also know that God sees all that happening here and what's in our hearts. The Bible also tells us to pray during all occasions, with all types of requests, and at the same time to give thanksgiving and praise. What does that look like when your world is caving in?

The Book of Psalms has many great examples of prayer—prayers of praise and prayer during times of trouble. For example, Psalm 56 was written by David, during a time when he was captured by the Philistines. It represents an amazing example of how he trusted in God despite the adversity going on around him. There are also times, however, when it is difficult to put into words what to pray for. Yet in Romans 8:26 (KJV), we find, "Likewise the Spirit also helpeth our infirmities: for we know not what we should pray for as we ought: but the Spirit itself maketh intercession for us with groanings which cannot be uttered." In Matthew 6:8, Jesus tells us, "For your Father knows the things you have need of before you ask Him."

In other places in the Bible there are reassuring Scriptures that let us know we can go to the Lord with any difficulties. For example, Isaiah 25:4 tells us, "For You have been a strength to the poor, a strength to the needy in his distress, a refuge from the storm, a shade from the heat; for the blast of the terrible ones is as a storm against the wall." In Proverbs 18:10 (KJV), this same idea is reinforced: "The name of the Lord is a strong tower: the righteous runneth into it, and is safe." Psalm 61:3 builds on this same imagery of shelter and a strong tower. Isaiah 61:1 also mentions how Christ was sent to "heal the brokenhearted" and Psalm 147:3 echoes this by stating, "He heals the brokenhearted and binds up their wounds."

Shipwrecked

One last "storm" example from Scripture comes to mind when discussing weather and the Bible. In Acts chapter 27, Paul and several other prisoners under Roman guard set sail for Rome. Here, Paul was to testify before Caesar, and Luke, being his travelling companion, chronicled the journey. In verses 12 through 26, we learn how their ship got trapped in a storm, and from verses 27 through 44, we learn of their shipwreck due to the weather.

Their ship had been caught up in a storm, called a "northeaster", which caused them to lose sight of the sun and the stars for several days in a row. The storm was so bad that they had to throw cargo overboard along with some of the ship's tackle. Although Paul had warned them of disaster before they even left port, the centurion in charge of Paul's custody listened instead to the ship's pilot and the owner of the ship.

One night during the storm, however, God gave Paul a vision that they would survive and that indeed Paul would still stand before Caesar in Rome. At the time many of them had been starving for lack of food, but now Paul encouraged them to eat, reminding them of his own faith in God and God's promise. During a meal, Paul broke bread and gave thanks to God in front of everyone.

The next day, the ship ran aground on a sandbar. Some of the soldiers aboard wanted to kill Paul and the other prisoners, but the centurion in charge stopped them. From there, they went ashore and eventually were able to make their way to Rome. The key point here is that all of them survived—just as God had promised Paul—but they had to listen to God in order to make it. It's interesting to note, too, that Paul had some prior knowledge that at least he was going to survive. Back in Acts 23:11, Jesus himself told Paul that he must testify in Rome, just as he had done in Jerusalem.

Now Paul could have easily given up, especially when they could no longer see land or even navigate by the sun or stars. Yet there was

Paul, going on a few words from the Lord, breaking bread and giving thanks in the middle of a violent storm that threatened their lives.

Personally, I've seen God do this type of thing more than once as a sort of "pre-emptive" strike right before some bad news came or when a rough patch of life was just ahead. Numerous times God has given me and others particular pieces of Scripture to hang on to in difficult times, and many times it was the same verse given repeatedly in a one-week period through a wide variety of sources (books, sermons, radio broadcasts, personal Bible study time, etc.). In other situations, I had a friend call up with a Bible verse right before I received some bad news from another source.

Will God guide you through the storms of life and truly be a strong tower and a safe refuge? Yes, if you let Him. Another aspect to keep in mind is the power of praise amidst difficult circumstances. Although I'm at a loss how to explain it, God truly works in some amazing and breakthrough ways especially when times are tough and the last thing a person feels like doing is praising God. At these times, too, the praise can truly be a sacrifice. Yet despite our circumstances, God is still God, still in charge of the universe, and freely willing to give the "peace of God, which passeth all understanding." (Philippians 4:7, KJV)

Bibliography

Chapter One

"Flash Facts About Lightning." *National Geographic News*, June 24, 2005.
http://news.nationalgeographic.com/news/2004/06/0623_040623_ligh tningfacts.html

Lisa Levitt Ryckman, "The Great Locust Mystery." *Denver Rocky Mountain News*, June 22, 1999. Accessed March 26, 2012.
http://denver.rockymountainnews.com/millennium/0622mile.shtml

Carol Kaesuk Yoon, "Looking Back at the Days of the Locust." *The New York Times,* April 23, 2002. Accessed March 26, 2012.
http://www.nytimes.com/2002/04/23/science/looking-back-at-the-days-of-the-locust.html?pagewanted=all&src=pm

Chapter Two

Merrill C. Tenney and Moises Silva, editors. *The Zondervan Encyclopedia of the Bible*, Volume 4 (M-P), 2009. pg. 901-2.

Chapter Three

Jack Williams, *The AMS Weather Book: The Ultimate Guide to America's Weather*. University of Chicago Press, 2009. pg. 193.

Chapter Five

"August 19, 2009: Multiple Tornadoes Across the Area, Including in Minneapolis." National Weather Service. Accessed March 14, 2012.

http://www.crh.noaa.gov/images/mpx/StormReports/19August2009.pdf

Chapter Six

Anthony Watts, "On This July 4th, thank climate disruption for saving the USA in 1814." *Watts Up With That?*, July 4, 2011. Accessed March 20, 2012. http://wattsupwiththat.com/2011/07/04/on-this-july-4th-thank-climate-disruption-for-saving-the-usa-in-1814

"Dunkirk Evacuation", www.wikipedia.com, Accessed March 26, 2012. http://en.wikipedia.org/wiki/Dunkirk_evacuation

Chapter Seven

Richard D. Knabb, Jamie R. Rhome, and Daniel P. Brown. "Tropical Cyclone Report: Hurricane Katrina." National Hurricane Center website, December 20, 2005. Accessed March 26, 2012. http://www.nhc.noaa.gov/pdf/TCR-AL122005_Katrina.pdf

Aaron Klein, "Did God Send Katrina as Judgment for Gaza?" www.wnd.com, September 7, 2005. Accessed March 26, 2012. http://www.wnd.com/2005/09/32196

Jack Williams, *The AMS Weather Book: The Ultimate Guide to America's Weather*. University of Chicago Press, 2009. pg. 188.

Chapter Eight

"Irony alert: The unusually chilly global-warming summit." *The Week,* December 9, 2010. Accessed April 4, 2012. http://theweek.com/article/index/210181/irony-alert-the-unusually-chilly-global-warming-summit

Juliet Eilperin, "Post Carbon: Cancun talks start with call to the gods." *Washington Post*, November 29, 2010. Accessed March 26, 2012. http://voices.washingtonpost.com/post-carbon/2010/11/cancun_talks_start_with_a_call.html

Jonathan DuHamel, "Cancun Climate Conference, Japan says no to Kyoto." *Tucson Citizen*, December 8, 2010. Accessed March 26, 2012.
http://tucsoncitizen.com/wryheat/2010/12/08/cancun-climate-conference-japan-says-no-to-kyoto/

Steve Connor, "Vast methane 'plumes' seen in Arctic ocean as sea ice retreats." *The Independent*, December 13, 2011. Accessed March 26, 2012.
http://www.independent.co.uk/news/science/vast-methane-plumes-seen-in-arctic-ocean-as-sea-ice-retreats-6276278.html

Bill Gates, "Bill Gates on Energy: Innovating to Zero!" www.ted.com, February 2010. Accessed March 27, 2012.
http://www.ted.com/talks/bill_gates.html

"Great Pacific Garbage Patch", www.wikipedia.com. Accessed March 26, 2012.
http://en.wikipedia.org/wiki/Great_Pacific_Garbage_Patch

About the Author

Michael Galloway is an outdoors enthusiast whose interests include camping, fishing, hiking, writing, and technology. He has a degree in Journalism, and has been writing software in one language or another for over twenty years. He currently lives in Minnesota with his family.

* * *

Also by Michael Galloway

An Echo Through the Trees
Theft at the Speed of Light
Horizons
Corridors
Fractal Standard Time
Ionotatron
Chronopticus Rising
The Chronopticus Chronicles Series
Race the Sky
The Hammer of Amalynth
Windows Out
The Fire and the Anvil
Gathering the Artists